HAL LEONARD
STUDENT
PIANO
LIBRARY

More Christmas Piano Solos

For All Piano Methods

D0504036

Table of Contents

Book: ISBN 978-1-4234-8365-6
Book/CD: ISBN 978-1-4234-9330-3

HAL•LEONARD®
CORPORATION

7777 W. BLUEMOUND RD. P.O. BOX 13819 MILWAUKEE, WI 53213

Visit Hal Leonard Online at
www.halleonard.com

Christmas Time Is Here

from A CHARLIE BROWN CHRISTMAS

Words by Lee Mendelson
Music by Vince Guaraldi
Arranged by Phillip Keveren

Yule - tide by the fire - side and joy - ful mem - 'ries there.

mf

rit.

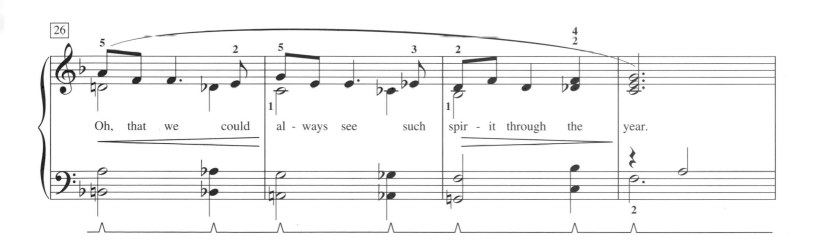

Christ-mas time is here, we'll be draw-ing near.

mp
a tempo

Oh, that we could al - ways see such spir - it through the year.

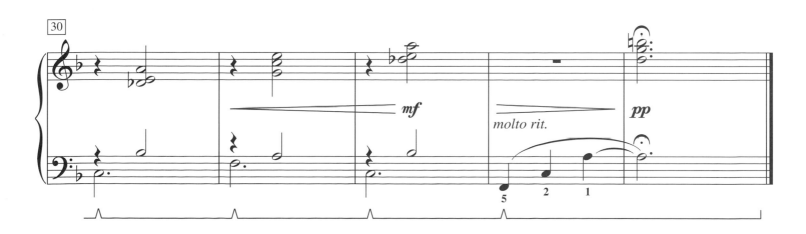

mf
molto rit.
pp

O Little Town of Bethlehem

Words by Phillips Brooks
Music by Lewis H. Redner
Arranged by Mona Rejino

in thy dark streets shin - eth the ev - er - last - ing
morn - ing stars, to - geth - er pro - claim the ho - ly

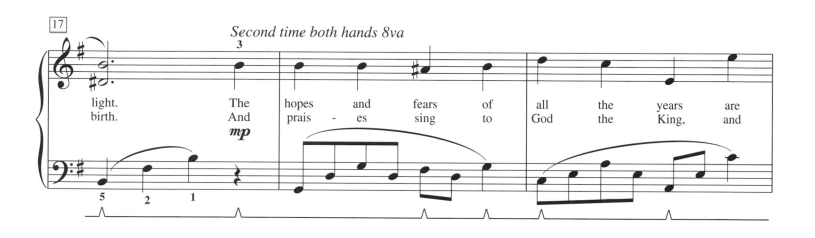

Second time both hands 8va

light. The hopes and fears of all the years are
birth. And prais - es sing to God the King, and

mp

1.
2.   *loco*

met in thee to - night. For
peace to men on   earth!

p

rit.

pp

5

White Christmas
from the Motion Picture Irving Berlin's HOLIDAY INN

Words and Music by
Irving Berlin
Arranged by Phillip Keveren

Brightly, with sparkle (♩ = 160)   TRACKS 5/6

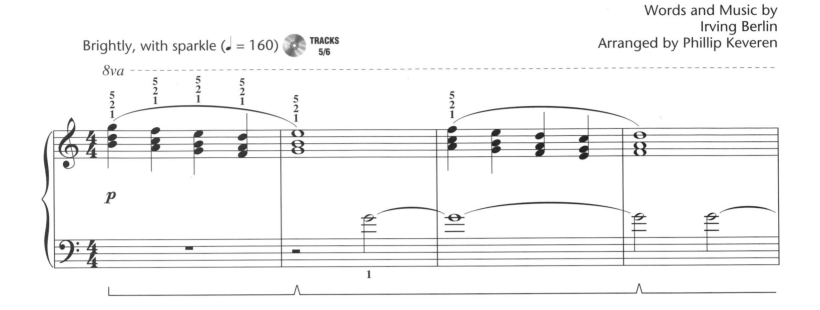

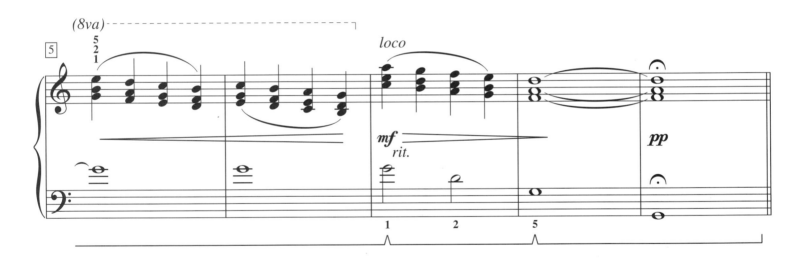

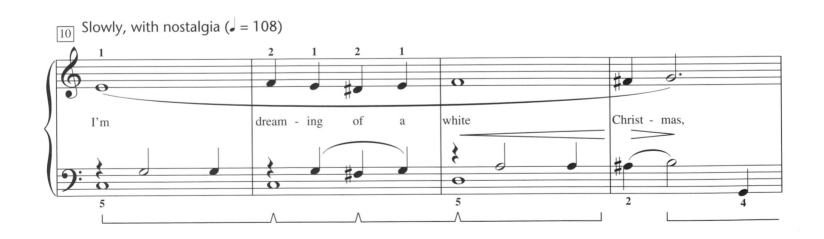

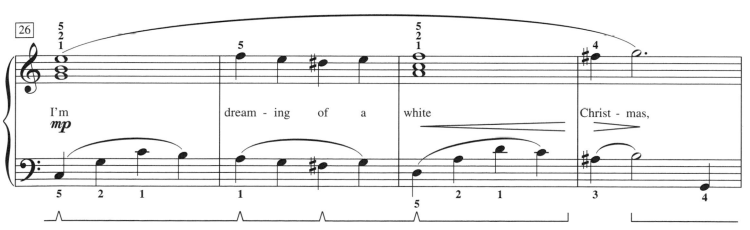

Jesu, Joy of Man's Desiring

from CANTATA NO. 147

By Johann Sebastian Bach
Arranged by Fred Kern

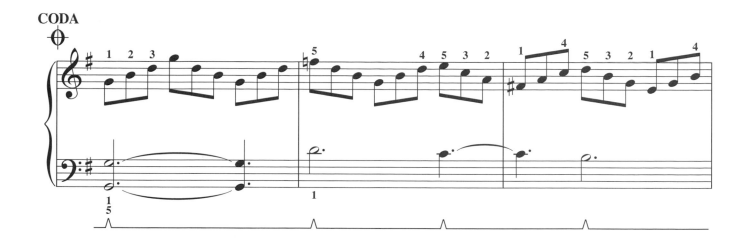

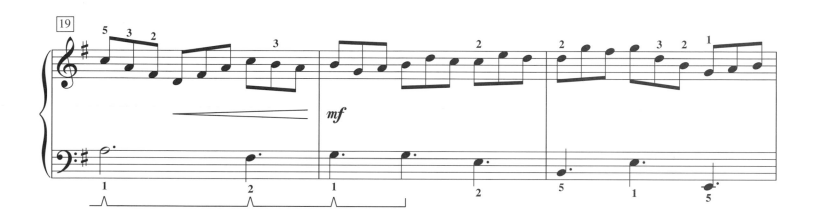

11

Skating

By Vince Guaraldi
Arranged by Phillip Keveren

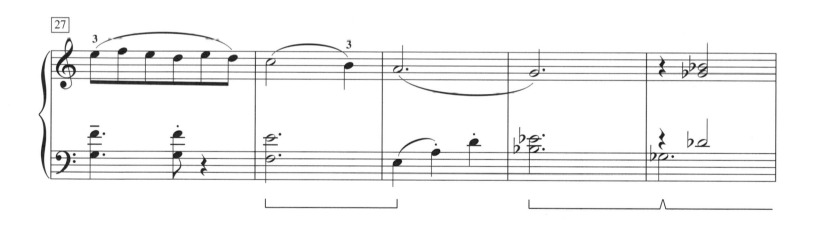

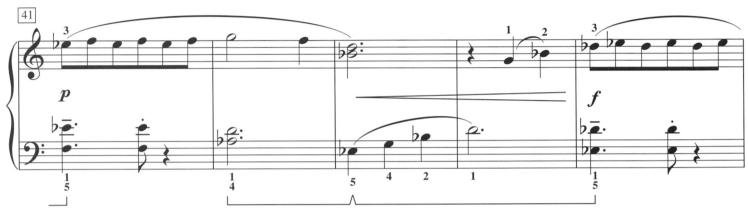

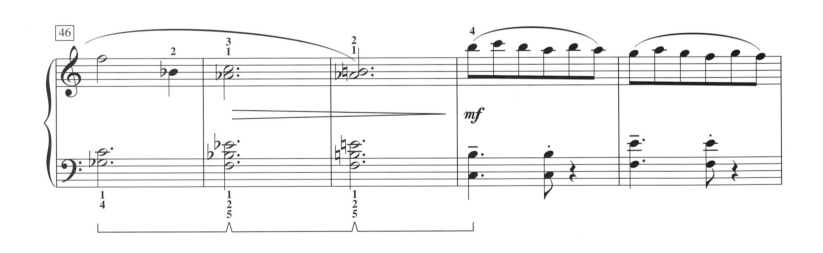

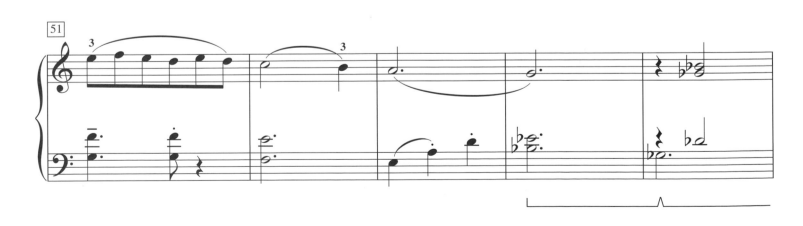

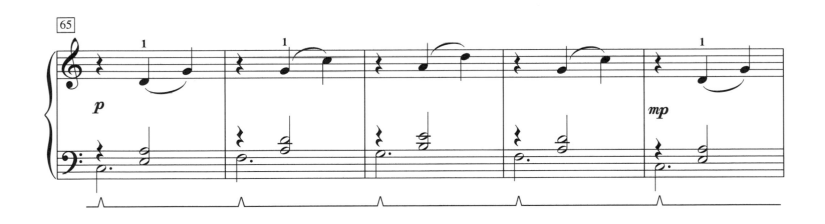

Somewhere in My Memory

from the Twentieth Century Fox Motion Picture HOME ALONE

Words by Leslie Bricusse
Music by John Williams
Arranged by Mona Rejino

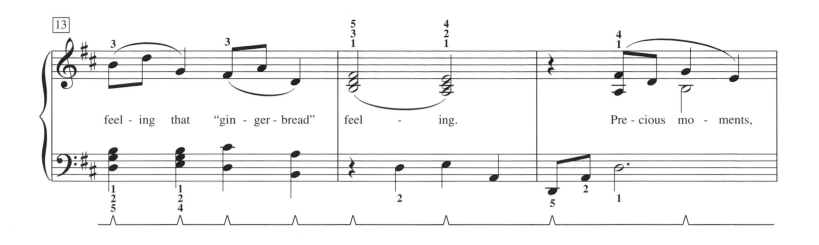

feel - ing that "gin - ger - bread" feel - ing. Pre - cious mo - ments,

simile spe - cial peo - ple, hap - py fac - es I can see.

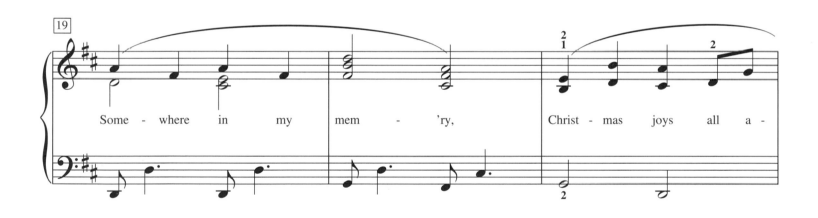

Some - where in my mem - 'ry, Christ - mas joys all a -

round me, liv - ing in my mem - 'ry.

All of the mu - sic, all of the mag - ic, all of the fam - 'ly

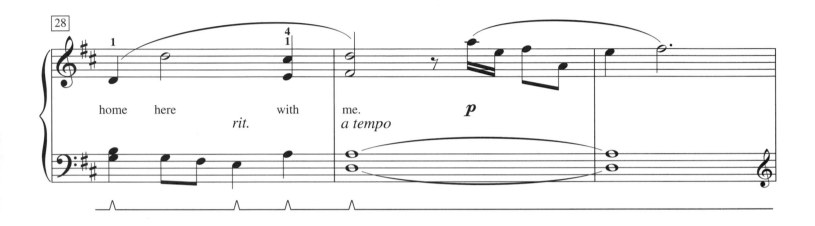

home here with me. *rit.* *a tempo* *p*

rit.

Carol of the Bells

Ukrainian Christmas Carol
Arranged by Carol Klose

Not too fast (♩ = 136) TRACKS 13/14

Optional: Beginning in m. 9, a second player may strike a triangle on beat one of every measure through m. 44.

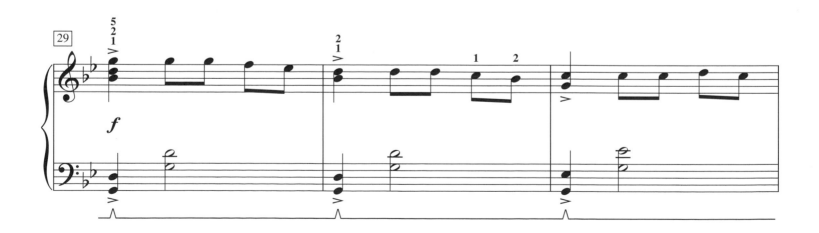

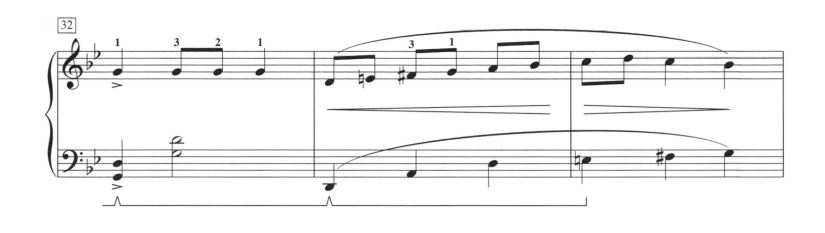

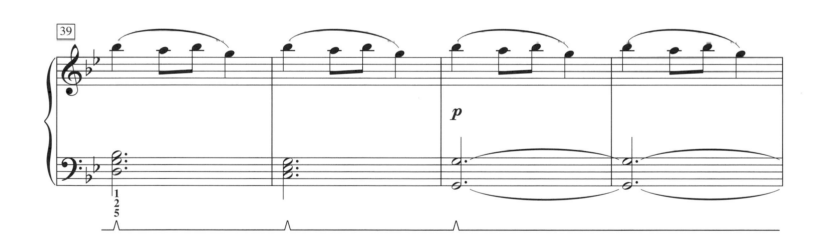

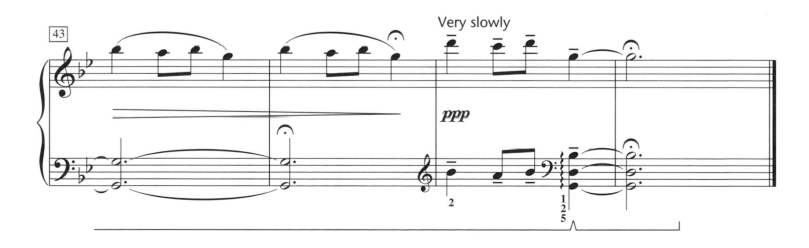

Where Are You Christmas?

from DR. SEUSS' HOW THE GRINCH STOLE CHRISTMAS

Words and Music by Will Jennings,
James Horner and Mariah Carey
Arranged by Fred Kern

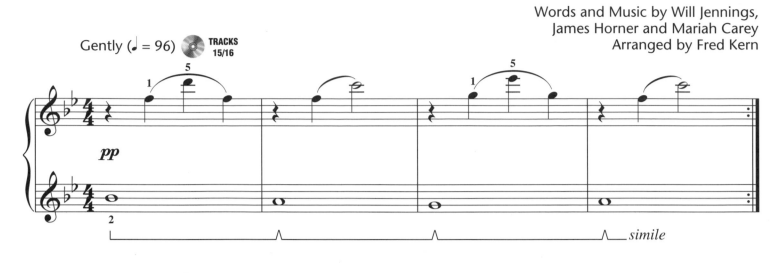

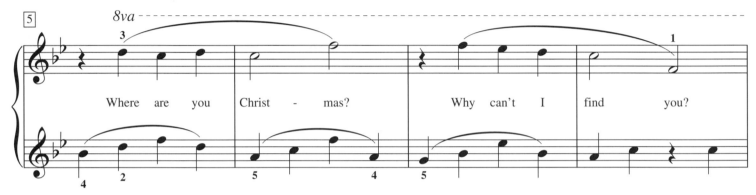

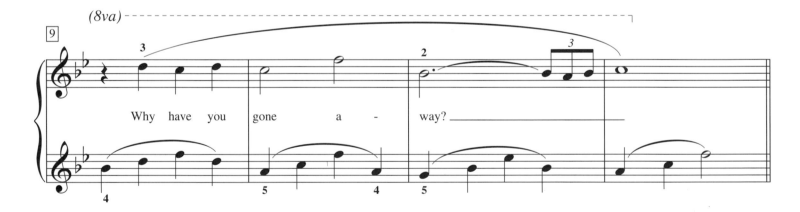

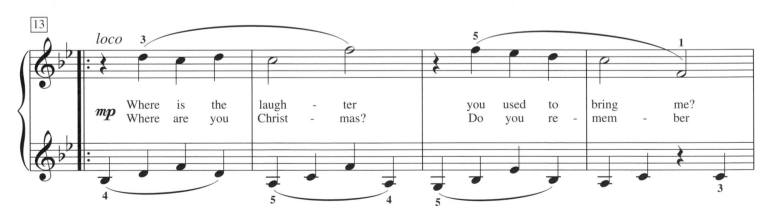

Why can't I hear mu - sic play? _____
the one you used to _____ know? _____

My world is chang - ing. ___ I'm re - ar - rang - ing.
I'm not the same one. ___ See what the time's done.

Does that mean Christ - mas chang _____ es
Is that why you ___ have let _____ me

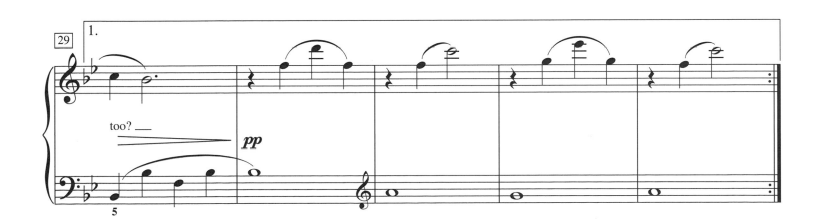

too? ___
pp

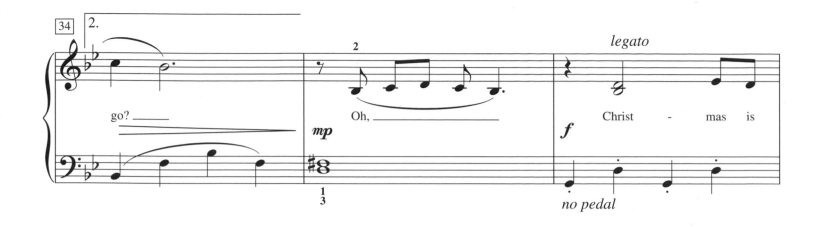

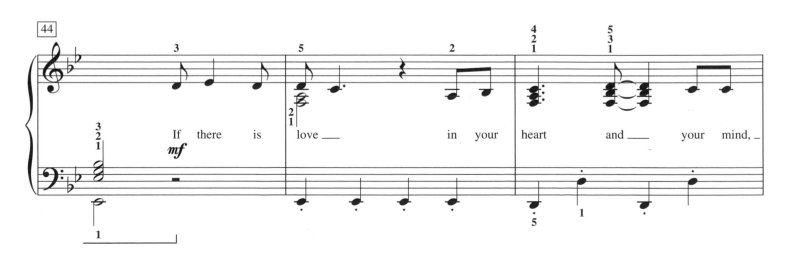

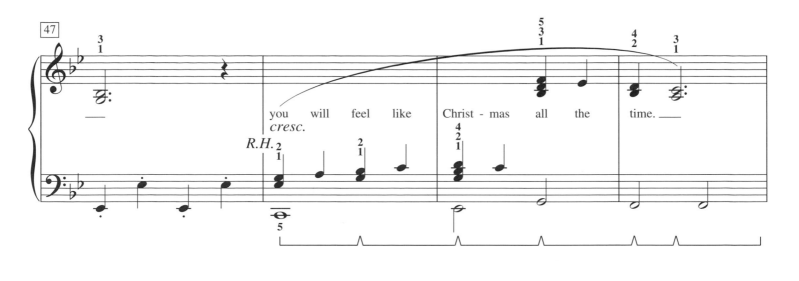

you will feel like Christ - mas all the time. ___

I feel you Christ - mas, ___ I know I

found you. You nev - er fade a - way. ___

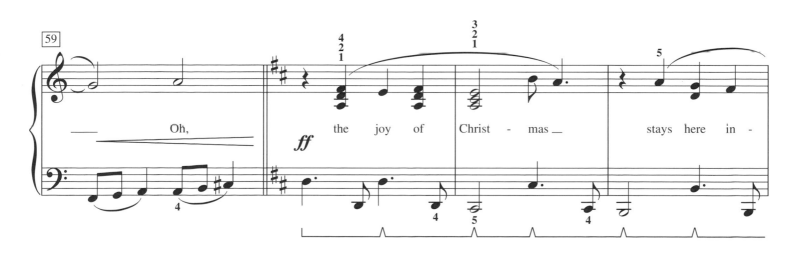

Oh, the joy of Christ - mas ___ stays here in -

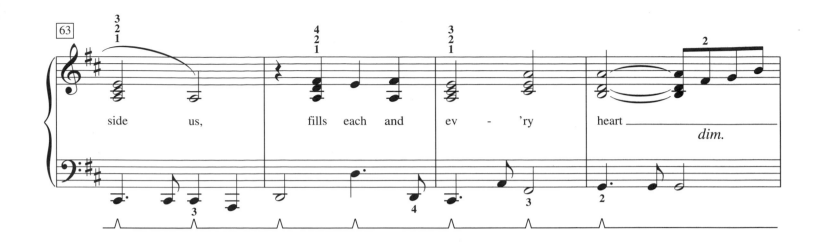

side us,   fills each and ev - 'ry   heart _____

dim.

_____ with love.

mp

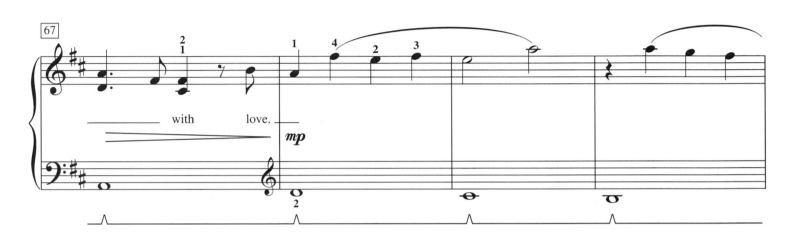

Where are you Christ - mas?

p

Fill your heart with love.

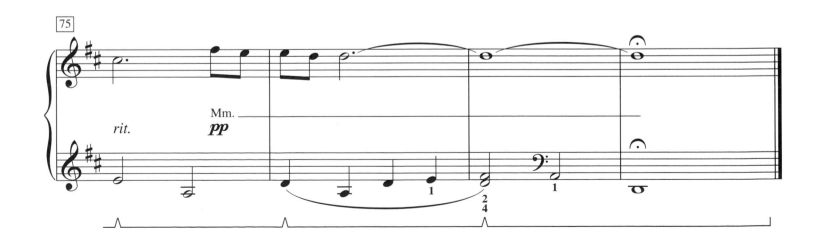

rit.   Mm. _____

pp

We Need a Little Christmas

from MAME

Music and Lyric by
Jerry Herman
Arranged by Carol Klose

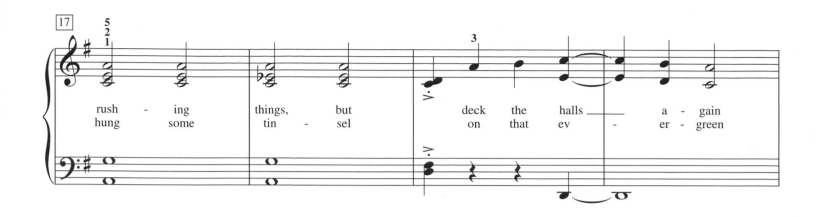

rush - ing things, but
hung some tin - sel

deck the halls _____ a - gain
on that ev - er - green

now. _____
bough. _____
cresc.

For we
For I've
f

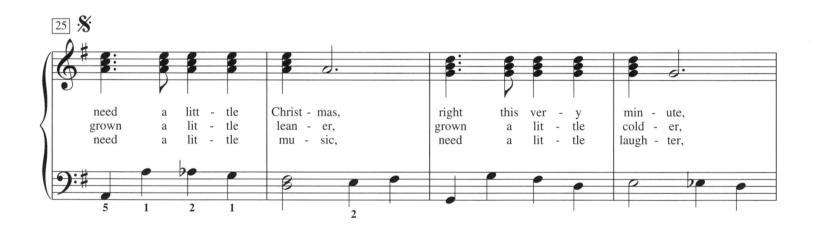

need a litt - tle Christ - mas,
grown a lit - tle lean - er,
need a lit - tle mu - sic,

right this ver - y min - ute,
grown a lit - tle cold - er,
need a lit - tle laugh - ter,

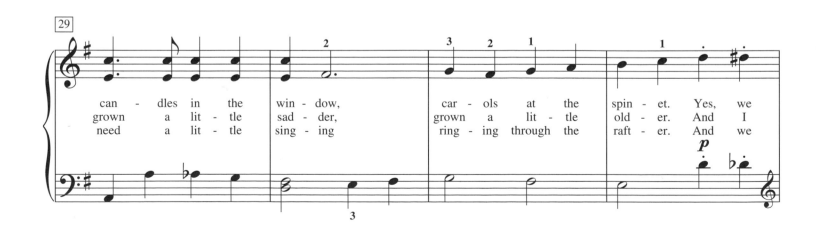

can - dles in the win - dow,
grown a lit - tle sad - der,
need a lit - tle sing - ing

car - ols at the spin - et. Yes, we
grown a lit - tle old - er. And I
ring - ing through the raft - er. And we
p

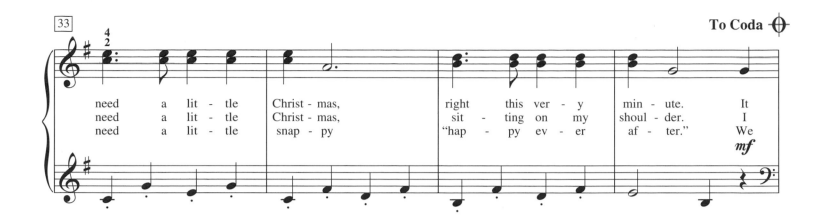

need   a   lit – tle   Christ – mas,   right   this   ver – y   min – ute.   It
need   a   lit – tle   Christ – mas,   sit – ting   on   my   shoul – der.   I
need   a   lit – tle   snap – py   "hap – py   ev – er   af – ter."   We

mf

1.

has – n't snowed a   sin – gle flur – ry, but   San – ta,   dear, we're   in   a   hur – ry. So

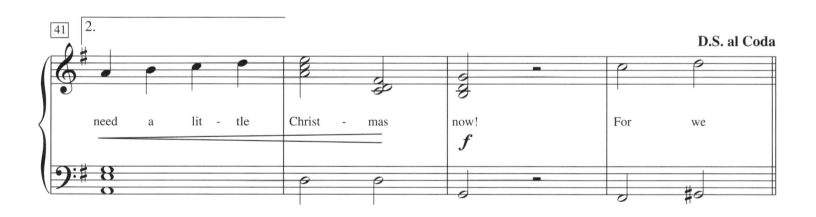

2.   **D.S. al Coda**

need   a   lit – tle   Christ – mas   now!   For   we

f

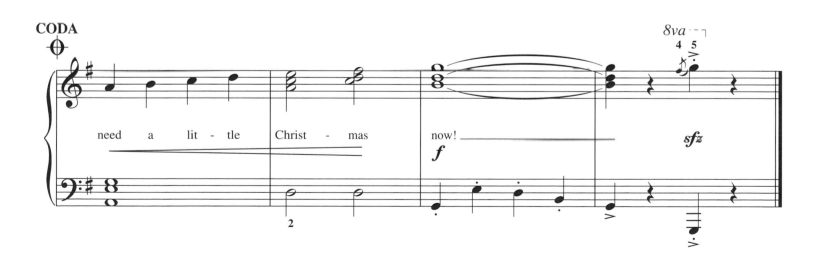

CODA
⊕

need   a   lit – tle   Christ – mas   now! _____

f   *sfz*

8va

Auld Lang Syne

Words by Robert Burns
Traditional Scottish Melody
Arranged by Phillip Keveren

Auld _____ Lang _____ Syne we'll take a cup of kind - ness yet for _____ Auld _____ Lang _____ Syne.

CELEBRATE THE HOLIDAYS WITH THE
HAL LEONARD STUDENT PIANO LIBRARY

Christmas Piano Solos

Favorite carols and seasonal songs, many with great teacher accompaniments! Instrumental accompaniments are also available on CD and GM disk. Arranged by Fred Kern, Phillip Keveren, Mona Rejino and Bruce Berr.

Level 1
00296049	Book Only	$6.99
00296081	CD Only	$10.95
00296101	GM Disk Only	$12.95

Level 2
00296050	Book Only	$6.99
00296082	CD Only	$10.95
00296102	GM Disk Only	$12.95

Level 3
00296051	Book Only	$6.95
00296083	CD Only	$10.95
00296103	GM Disk Only	$12.95

Level 4
00296052	Book Only	$6.95
00296084	CD Only	$10.95
00296104	GM Disk Only	$12.95

Level 5
00296146	Book Only	$6.95
00296159	CD Only	$10.95
00296162	GM Disk Only	$12.95

Christmas Piano Ensembles

Four-part student ensembles arranged for two or more pianos by Phillip Keveren. Featuring favorite Christmas carols and hymns in graded books that correspond directly to the five levels of the Hal Leonard Student Piano Library. CD and GM disk accompaniments are available separately.

Level 1
00296338	Book Only	$6.95
00296343	CD Only	$10.95
00296348	GM Disk Only	$12.95

Level 2
00296339	Book Only	$6.95
00296344	CD Only	$10.95
00296349	GM Disk Only	$12.95

Level 3
00296340	Book Only	$6.95
00296345	CD Only	$10.95
00296350	GM Disk Only	$12.95

Level 4
00296341	Book Only	$6.95
00296346	CD Only	$10.95
00296351	GM Disk Only	$12.95

Level 5
00296342	Book Only	$6.95
00296347	CD Only	$10.95
00296352	GM Disk Only	$12.95

More Christmas Piano Solos

Following up on the success of the Christmas Piano Solos books for levels 1-5 in the Hal Leonard Student Piano Library, these books contain additional holiday selections for each grade level that will work great with any piano method. Each song includes an optional teacher accompaniment. Arranged by Fred Kern, Phillip Keveren, Carol Klose, Jennifer Linn and Mona Rejino.

Pre-Staff
00296790	Book Only	$6.99

Level 1
00296791	Book Only	$6.99

Level 2
00296792	Book Only	$6.99

Level 3
00296793	Book Only	$6.99

Level 4
00296794	Book Only	$7.99

Level 5
00296795	Book Only	$7.99

Festive Chanukah Songs – Level 2
arranged by Bruce Berr

7 solos with teacher accompaniments: Candle Blessings • Chanukah • Come Light The Menorah • Hanérot, Halalu • The Dreydl Song • S'vivon • Ma'oz Tsur.

00296194		$5.95

Festive Songs for the Jewish Holidays – Level 3
arranged by Bruce Berr

11 solos, some with teacher accompaniments: Who Can Retell? • Come Light The Menorah • S'vivon • Ma'oz Tsur • I Have A Little Dreydl • Dayénu • Adir Hu • Eliyahu Hanavi • Chad Gadya • Hatikvah.

00296195		$6.99

FOR MORE INFORMATION, SEE YOUR LOCAL MUSIC DEALER,
OR WRITE TO:

HAL•LEONARD® CORPORATION
7777 W. BLUEMOUND RD. P.O. BOX 13819 MILWAUKEE, WI 53213

www.halleonard.com

Prices, contents, and availability subject to change without notice. Some products may not be available outside the U.S.A.